SNOOPY

(features as)

The Music Lover

Charles M. Schulz

ЯR

PEANUTS is a registered trademark of United Feature Syndicate, Inc.
Based on the PEANUTS® comic strip by Charles M. Schulz.

Originally published in 1990 as 'Snoopy Stars as Ludwig Van Beagle'.
This edition published in the Year 2001 by Ravette Publishing.

Printed and bound in Great Britain
for Ravette Publishing Limited,
Unit 3, Tristar Centre,
Star Road, Partridge Green,
West Sussex RH13 8RA
by Cox & Wyman, Berkshire

ISBN: 1 84161 106 9

YOU KNOW WHY? BECAUSE YOU DON'T CARE ANYTHING ABOUT BEETHOVEN! YOU NEVER HAVE!!

YOU DON'T CARE THAT HE SUFFERED! YOU DON'T CARE THAT HIS STOMACH HURT AND THAT HE COULDN'T HEAR!

YOU NEVER CARED THAT THE COUNTESS TURNED HIM DOWN, OR THAT THERESE MARRIED THE BARON INSTEAD OF HIM OR THAT LOBKOWITZ STOPPED HIS ANNUITY!!

12-15

IF THE COUNTESS HADN'T TURNED HIM DOWN, WOULD YOU BUY ME SOMETHING?

I HAVE A QUESTION I'D LIKE TO ASK YOU..

WHAT MAKES YOU THINK BEETHOVEN WAS BETTER THAN ELTON JOHN?

4-6

10-26

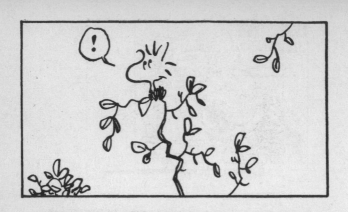

7-31

4-28

4-26

9-10

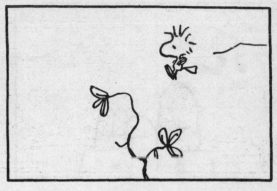

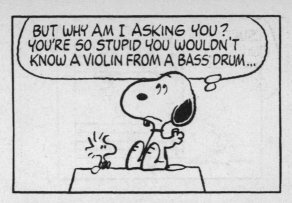

2-18

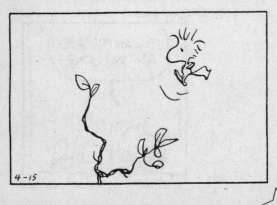

4-15

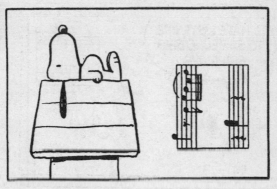

12-27

S-3

© 1984 United Feature Syndicate, Inc.

© 1983 United Feature Syndicate, Inc.

9-18

3-31

Schulz

I BROUGHT SOME OF MY VACATION PICTURES FOR YOU TO SEE, SCHROEDER, BUT I GUESS YOU'RE BUSY...

WHY DON'T I JUST LEAVE THEM HERE, AND YOU CAN LOOK AT THEM LATER?

YOU WERE RIGHT...THE LID WAS OFF THE JAR.

NO ONE CAN SLEEP WITH A BUNCH OF CHOCOLATE CHIP COOKIES SINGING ALL NIGHT..

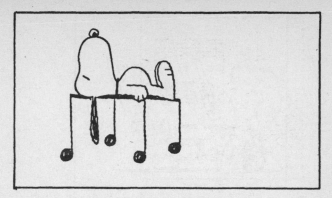

9-14

10-10 © 1989 United Feature Syndicate, Inc.

10-11 © 1989 United Feature Syndicate, Inc.

Other PEANUTS titles published by Ravette ...

Snoopy Pocket Books

Snoopy features as ...	ISBN	Price
Man's Best Friend	1 84161 066 6	£2.99
Master of the Fairways	1 84161 067 4	£2.99
The Fearless Leader	1 84161 104 2	£2.99
The Fitness Fanatic	1 84161 029 1	£2.99
The Flying Ace	1 84161 027 5	£2.99
The Great Philosopher	1 84161 064 X	£2.99
The Legal Beagle	1 84161 065 8	£2.99
The Literary Ace	1 84161 026 7	£2.99
The Master Chef	1 84161 107 7	£2.99
The Matchmaker	1 84161 028 3	£2.99
The Sportsman	1 84161 105 0	£2.99

Peanuts 'Little Book' series

	ISBN	Price
Charlie Brown - Wisdom	1 84161 099 2	£2.50
Snoopy - Laughter	1 84161 100 X	£2.50
Lucy - Advice	1 84161 101 8	£2.50
Peppermint Patty - Blunders	1 84161 102 6	£2.50

	ISBN	Price
Peanuts Anniversary Treasury	1 84161 021 6	£9.99
Peanuts Treasury	1 84161 043 7	£9.99

	ISBN	Price
You Really Don't Look 50 Charlie Brown	1 84161 020 8	£7.99

Snoopy's Laughter and Learning series
wipe clean pages
(a fun series of story and activity books for preschool and infant school children)

	ISBN	Price
Book 1 - Read With Snoopy	1 84161 016 X	£2.50
Book 2 - Write With Snoopy	1 84161 017 8	£2.50
Book 3 - Count With Snoopy	1 84161 018 6	£2.50
Book 4 - Colour With Snoopy	1 84161 019 4	£2.50

All PEANUTS™ books are available from your local bookshop or from the address below. Just tick the titles required and send the form with your payment to:-

BBCS, P.O. Box 941, Kingston upon Hull HU1 3YQ
24-hr telephone credit card line 01482 224626

Prices and availability are subject to change without prior notice.

Please enclose a cheque or postal order made payable to BBCS to the value of the cover price of the book and allow the following for postage and packing:-

UK & BFPO:	£1.95 (weight up to 1kg)		3-day delivery
	£2.95 (weight over 1kg up to 20kg)		3-day delivery
	£4.95 (weight up to 20kg)		next day delivery
EU & Eire:	Surface Mail:	£2.50 for first book & £1.50 for subsequent books	
	Airmail:	£4.00 for first book & £2.50 for subsequent books	
USA:	Surface Mail:	£4.50 for first book & £2.50 for subsequent books	
	Airmail:	£7.50 for first book & £3.50 for subsequent books	
Rest of the World:	Surface Mail:	£6.00 for first book & £3.50 for subsequent books	
	Airmail:	£10.00 for first book & £4.50 for subsequent books	

Name: ....

Address: ....

....

....

Cards accepted: Visa, Mastercard, Switch, Delta, American Express

Expiry date .... Signature ....